•••◦◉ *BULLETPOINTS* ◉◦•••

ARACHNIDS

Consultant: Barbara Taylor

Miles Kelly

PUBLISHING

First published in 2005 by Miles Kelly Publishing Ltd
Bardfield Centre, Great Bardfield
Essex, CM7 4SL

Some of this material also appears in the *1000 Facts* series and the *Visual Factfinder* series

2 4 6 8 10 9 7 5 3 1

Editorial Director: Belinda Gallagher

Editorial Assistant: Amanda Askew

Picture researcher: Liberty Newton

Production: Estela Boulton

Scanning and reprographics: Anthony Cambray, Mike Coupe, Ian Paulyn

British Library Cataloguing-in-Publication Data
A catalogue record for this book is available from the British Library

ISBN 1-84236-550-9

Printed in China

www.mileskelly.net
info@mileskelly.net

Acknowledgements
p. 37 Derek Bromhall/ Oxford Scientific/photolibrary
p. 38 John Cook/Oxford Scientific/photolibrary

Contents

Arachnids

▶ *An imperial scorpion. Although they are a widespread group of invertebrates, most arachnids are terrestrial (live on land). Scorpions are most commonly found in warm countries.*

- **Arachnids** include a variety of creatures, such as spiders, scorpions, ticks, mites, harvestmen and schizomids. Fossils of arachnids suggest that they were among the first land inhabitants of this planet. These creatures can be found anywhere but they are most common in dry and tropical regions.

- **Arachnids** have eight legs. They also have two pairs of appendages (the chelicerae and the pedipalps) at the front of the body, which are used to grasp and hold prey.

- **Arachnids** are classified as invertebrates.

- **Diverse in size**, they can range from a few millimetres to more than 20 cm in length. They have a segmented body, a hard exoskeleton to protect them from enemies. The exoskeleton is a shell made of carbohydrates and calcium.

- **An arachnid's body** is divided into two parts: the cephalothorax (joint head and thorax) and the abdomen. The cephalothorax has sensory organs, mouthparts, stomach and limbs, while the abdomen contains the heart, lungs, gut, reproductive organs and anus.

- **Arachnids** do not have teeth and jaws to chew their food and most can not digest food. This is why they suck fluids from their prey's body.

- **Instead of having lungs**, arachnids have two types of breathing mechanism – book lungs and tracheae.

- **The legs** of an arachnid are sometimes used for catching and holding enemies.

- **Sensory hairs**, simple eyes and slit sensory organs are used to sense the surroundings.

- **Arachnids** are cold-blooded creatures and get warmth from their environment.

Spiders

- **Spiders** belong to the family Araneae within the class Arachnida.

- **The body** of a spider is divided into two distinct parts – the cephalothorax (joined head and thorax) and abdomen. A slender stalk connects these two body parts. This is known as the pedicel.

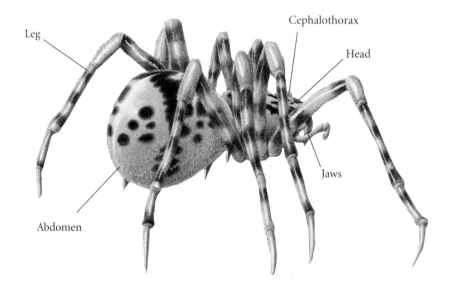

Leg

Cephalothorax

Head

Jaws

Abdomen

▲ *Most spiders catch their prey by spinning webs or hunting. The unique spitting spider catches its prey by squirting a sticky substance at it.*

- **The cephalothorax** of a spider is known as the prosoma. The legs, eyes, stomach and brain are situated in the prosoma. The prosoma is covered by a hard exoskeleton.
- **Spiders** have 6 to 8 simple eyes. There are two types of eyes – black or diurnal eyes, and white or nocturnal eyes.
- **The nervous system** is a bunch of nerves in the cephalothorax. Spiders are hairy creatures. These hairs are sensitive to even a slight breeze. A spider's hairs are connected to its nervous system and work as sensory organs.
- **Most spiders** breathe with the help of two pairs of lungs known as book lungs. These are simple breathing tubes. Some spiders only have one pair of book lungs.
- **The abdomen** of a spider is called the opisthosoma. This body segment contains the reproductive organs, heart and silk glands. The abdomen also has a protective covering.
- **Spiders have four pairs** of legs attached to the prosoma. Each of the legs has seven segments. The first pair of legs are often used as sensory feelers by spiders. All the legs have at least one claw at the tip.
- **A spider has** a total of six pairs of appendages on its body. The first is a pair of jaws (chelicerae). These jaws are connected to venom-producing glands and can be used in self-defence and for hunting prey. Males carry sperm cells in the second pair of appendages (pedipalps). Females use their pedipalps to hold food material. The remaining four pairs of appendages are walking legs.
- **Blood** flows freely within a spider's body. This is a similar blood system to that of an insect. However, some spiders also have veins and arteries to carry blood all over the body.

Orb-web spider

- **Orb-web spiders** are named after the orb-shaped webs they spin to trap their prey. These spiders are also called orb-web weavers.

- **They are the largest** web-weaving spiders. The webs vary greatly in size and structural design. Some species decorate the webs with extra silk.

- **Only the females** weave webs. Most build a new web every night. They build their nests in open areas and between flower stems. It usually takes an hour to build a web.

- **A thin**, sticky thread is released to start making the web. This thread is carried by the wind and when it sticks to something, the spider walks along the thread to make it thicker. This is repeated until a strong web is ready.

- **These spiders** are found in a variety of sizes and colours. They usually have hairy bodies and legs. Their hair helps them to sense any activity around them.

- **Although** most orb-web spiders are blind or have very weak eyesight, they can distinguish between day and night.

- **There are many kinds** of orb-web spiders. Some of the most common are the golden orb weaver, the St. Andrew's cross spider and the cross or garden spider.

- **Male orb-web spiders** pluck strands of the web to attract the attention of the females. Females are usually larger than the males.

- **When prey** is trapped in the web, the spider wraps it in a sticky silky substance so that it does not tear the web apart. The wrapped prey is then either eaten immediately or stored and eaten later.

- **When disturbed**, most orb web spiders fall to the ground in alarm. However, this is not true for all species. For instance, when a female St. Andrew's cross spider is disturbed, she grasps her web and shakes it.

▲ *The orb-web spider weaves a beautiful web shaped like a wheel. It has strong, straight threads and sticky spiral threads to catch prey, such as flies. About 4000 species of orb web spider have been identified so far. They are amongst the most common of all spiders and live in forests, gardens and grasslands worldwide.*

House spider

- **House spiders** are the most common spiders. They are easily spotted in houses and gardens. They are also found in woodpiles and under logs.

- **These spiders** have a yellowish brown body with grey and black markings on their abdomen. Females have yellow legs, while males have orange.

- **Males** are smaller than females but have longer legs. The leg span of males can be as long as 60 mm.

- **These spiders** feed on small invertebrates, such as beetles, cockroaches, earwigs and even earthworms.

- **Sometimes** house spiders can survive without food for months.

- **The webs** are constructed in the corners of rooms, under tables or chairs and in window frames.

- **The house spider builds** its sheet-shaped web and waits for its prey to become trapped.

- **During the mating process**, the male stays with the female for a few weeks and mates a couple of times. After mating, the male does not die. Sometimes the female spider eats the male after mating.

- **The egg sacs** are brown and have a hard, papery covering.

- **Some people** find the house spider irritating because it frequently spins new webs in different places and can produce many webs in a short time.

▲ *House spiders go on a night venture too near the edge of the bath and slide in by accident. House spiders and black widow spiders are closely related and belong to the same family, known as cobweb spiders. House spiders, however, are not dangerous.*

11

Black widow spider

- **Black widow spiders** are the most feared and dangerous spiders. Both male and female black widows are venomous. Their bite is fatal to humans.

- **A female's bite** is more poisonous than that of the male. The females are black and have a red hourglass mark on their abdomen.

- **The males** are tan and cream in colour and have red and yellow markings on their legs. They are smaller than the females.

- **Found** in the warm and temperate regions of the world, such as the United States, Italy and South Africa, these spiders live in dark places such as drainpipes or under rocks and wood. They are not usually found in houses.

- **Black widows eat** flies, moths and other small insects. These creatures are considered beneficial because they feed on cockroaches and crickets.

- **Deadly** black widow spiders prey on insects and other spiders, but their venom also works on vertebrates, such as mice.

- **The female black widow** constructs an irregular-shaped web, which is tangled. The core of the web is like a funnel to capture large insects.

- **Once prey** is captured, the female wraps it in silk and kills it by injecting venom. The venom digests the prey and the spider is able to eat it easily.

- **The female** lays her eggs in egg sacs. Each egg sac contains several hundred eggs. She stays near her eggs and guards them. During this period, the female is more likely to bite if disturbed.

- **After about 20 days**, the spiderlings emerge from the eggs by tearing the egg sac. The egg sacs contain poison but the spiderlings are not poisonous. However, they tend to be cannibalistic and eat each other.

▲ *After mating, the female black widow sometimes eats the male. She mates only once in her lifetime, which is why she's called a 'widow'. After mating, she stores the sperm in her body.*

Tarantula

▲ *A female tarantula guarding her eggs. The eggs are surrounded by a shell, or cocoon, of silk. Tarantulas are the world's largest spiders. Their bodies reach up to 12 cm long. One species – the Goliath bird-eater – is recorded as having a record-breaking leg span of 28 cm.*

- **Tarantulas** are hairy spiders found in the warm regions of the world, such as South America, southern parts of Asia and Africa.

- **Although they look** scary, they are not very harmful to humans, although their bite is venomous. These creatures have a two-part body, strong jaws to grasp their food and eight hairy legs. The body is protected with a hard exoskeleton.

- **The hairs** on a tarantula's body are sensitive to temperature, touch and smell. The barbed hairs on the abdomen come off easily.

- **Tarantulas usually** dig underground burrows but some live in burrows dug by rodents or other animals. Some species live on the ground or in trees.

- **Tarantulas** eat a variety of animals from insects and small reptiles to small birds and frogs.

- **Their powerful jaws** can be used to crush their prey.

- **Active at night**, tarantulas search for prey or wait outside their burrows for it to come near them. They kill it with their fangs. Then they inject a chemical to dissolve its flesh so that it becomes easy for them to eat.

- **The male** searches for a female by following the scent she produces. After performing the courtship dance, they mate. The female then lays her eggs in her burrow and weaves a cocoon to protect them.

- **The lifespan** of these spiders is longer than that of other spiders. Females can live for up to 20 years but males do not live as long.

- **When cornered**, tarantulas purr and raise their front legs in a defensive position.

Hunting spider

- **Hunting spiders**, such as water spiders and wolf spiders, are named after their habit of waiting for their prey and then pouncing on it.

- **Most species** do not construct webs to trap their prey.

- **Some of these spiders**, however, construct large webs on the ground and run after insects that land in the web.

- **Hunting spiders** that do not weave webs, spin a silken thread and hang from it. They can use these threads to descend to the ground from high places.

- **Large eyes** enable hunting spiders to see their prey from a considerable distance. However, crab spiders, water spiders and tarantulas have small eyes.

- **The strong chelicerae** (a pair of 'jaws' used for clasping and killing the prey) of hunting spiders help them to hunt and capture their victims.

- **The cephalothorax** (the fused head and thorax region) is usually larger in hunting spiders than in web-spinning spiders.

- **Hunting spiders** are similar in size and form to the giant crab spider.

- **They have flattened bodies** and legs that point forward to enable them to slip under loose bark or stones quickly and easily.

- **Vegetation** and tree trunks are the preffered habitats of hunting spiders.

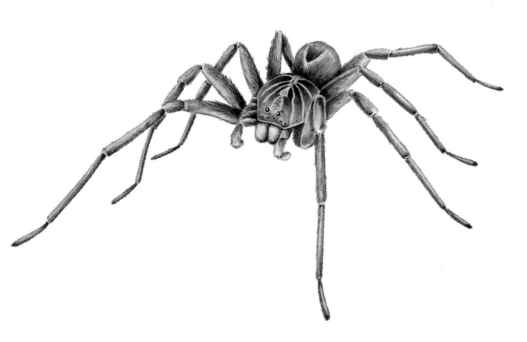

▲ *Hunting spiders such as this wolf spider have excellent eyesight that they can rely on to find and capture prey.*

Mouse spider

- **Mouse spiders** are so-called due to their grey stomachs covered with hair, which looks like mouse fur. These spiders are sometimes mistaken for funnel-web spiders.

- **These spiders** belong to the trapdoor family of spiders. The two main species are the red-headed mouse spider and the eastern mouse spider.

- **They range** in size from 1 to 3 cm. These spiders have short, stocky legs and many tiny eyes spread across their head.

- **These spiders** can be found in all kinds of habitats, ranging from deserts to rainforests.

- **They live** in oval burrows, which they dig in the ground. Hidden trapdoors cover these. After covering the walls of the burrows with digestive fluids and mud, the mouse spider lines the walls with silk.

- **The female spends** her entire life in the burrow but the male wanders freely. Mouse spiders feed mainly on insects but they are also known to eat frogs, lizards, mice, small birds and other spiders.

- **Mouse spiders** do not spin webs to catch their prey. Instead they usually hunt for them at night. Once caught, the victim is crushed and then immobilized with venom before the spider feeds.

- **Few males** escape alive after mating. The female lays the eggs in a place halfway down the burrow.

- **Once the spiderlings** hatch, they continue to share the burrow with their mother. By doing this, many spiderlings are able to survive.

- **When they are in danger**, these spiders are aggressive and usually rise up on their hind legs . They have large fangs, which can deliver painful and dangerous bites. They can pose a threat to humans.

▲ *A male red-headed mouse spider leaves its burrow. Females are smaller than males, and they are entirely black.*

Bird-eating spiders

▲ *Bird-eating spiders were originally named over 100 years ago, when witnesses reported that they had seen these creatures attacking birds.*

- **Bird-eating spiders** are very large. They are usually found in the tropics. There are around 600 species.

- **These spiders** have hair on their bodies and legs. They have four book lungs and spinnerets. Their jaws move vertically instead of sideways.

- **Although** mistakenly referred to as tarantulas, bird-eating spiders belong to a different family altogether.

- **Bird-eating spiders** come out to hunt at night. They do spin webs but usually chase their prey. They silently and suddenly dash to catch small mammals or drag hummingbirds from their nests.

- **Once prey** is captured, the spider stabs it with its sharp, pointed hollow fangs and injects venom. These spiders are not dangerous to human beings.

- **While mating**, the male approaches the female very cautiously to avoid being eaten by her.

- **The female** lays her eggs in a loose cocoon. She guards them by resting her front legs on them or by sitting on them. After three weeks, white spiderlings hatch from the eggs.

- **The spiderlings** stay in the cocoon for up to five weeks. When they leave the cocoon, they are brown with a black spot on the abdomen.

- **Adult spiders** have been known to survive without food for as long as two years. They can live for up to 17 years.

- **Bird-eating spiders** primarily feed on small birds, such as hummingbirds and warblers. Their main enemy is the hunting wasp.

Spitting spider

▲ *A spitting spider has silk glands, which are connected to its poison fangs. When it spots its prey, it spits a sticky silken substance over the prey to immobilize it.*

- **Spitting spiders belong** to the family of six-eyed spiders, Haplogynae. They have six eyes and long, thin legs.

- **It is believed** that spitting spiders originally came from the tropics. They are now found worldwide. In cooler climates they are most likely to be found inside buildings.

- **These spiders** are shiny and have a light brown body with black spots and legs with black rings. They are quite small, ranging from 3 to 6 mm. Spitting spiders have a distinctive shape – a large dome-shaped head and chest area (cephalothorax).

- **Found** all over the world, they live in dark corners of houses or around window frames and in cupboards. Sometimes they can be found outdoors under leaves and bark.

- **Spitting spiders** usually hunt at night. They do not have very good eyesight and rely on long sensory hairs on their legs to detect their prey.

- **Little is known** about the mating habits of these spiders.

- **After laying** her eggs, the female carries them around in her fangs. The eggs hatch about two weeks later.

- **Spitting spiders** have a relatively long life span and live for 2 to 4 years.

- **These spiders** are not harmful to human beings.

> **. . . FASCINATING FACT . . .**
> Spitting spiders feed on mosquitoes, moths and flies. They
> often swing their heads from side to side while spitting,
> creating a zigzag stream which binds the prey to the ground.

Raft spider

- **Raft spiders** belong to the order Araneae. They are dark brown with stripes on each side of the body. Raft spiders are not poisonous.

- **Males** measure 10 to 13 mm in length while females measure up to 22 mm.

- **Raft spiders** live near water and do not spin webs. They feed on tadpoles, small frogs and insects.

- **To locate its prey**, a raft spider lowers its front legs in the water and feels the vibrations. The spider then pulls its prey out of water and feeds on it.

- **Raft spiders** can crawl down water plants if threatened and can remain underwater for about an hour.

- **During courtship**, the male spider attracts the female by making regular waves on the surface of water. He jerks his abdomen up and down and waves his legs in the air.

- **The female** is very aggressive towards the male and in some cases she might even eat the courting male.

- **After mating**, the female lays more than 1000 eggs in a large egg sac.

- **The egg sac** is green in colour and is carried around by the female. When the spiderlings are about to emerge, the female spins a protective silk web around the egg sac. She opens the egg sac and guards it until the spiderlings emerge.

····· FASCINATING FACT ·····
The raft spider can walk on the water's surface
without sinking. It spreads its legs out wide and
takes quick, gentle steps.

▼ A raft spider waits patiently for the right time to strike. Its sensitive legs touch the water, feeling for any vibrations caused by possible prey, such as fish or frogs.

Scorpions

- **Scorpions** are feared by humans because of their deadly sting. Their grasping, pincer-like appendages can be a scary sight. They have been around for over 400 million years.

- **Easily identified** by their venomous tail at the end of an elongated body, they also have four pairs of legs and two lobster-like claws (pincers) called pedipalps. The average size of a scorpion is 6 cm.

- **The pincers** are used as weapons to catch prey. Scorpions grab their prey with their pincers . Then they use their sting to inject venom, which paralyzes their victim.

- **Scorpions** can be tan, red, black or brown in colour. A hard exoskeleton protects the scorpion from external damage.

- **The tiny sensory hairs** covering the body and legs helps scorpions to detect temperature changes and movement around them.

- **Scorpions** have book lungs, which are gilllike structures for breathing.

- **In extreme weather** conditions, the extra layer of fat under the scorpion's exoskeleton helps it to survive.

- **The sting** is normally used to paralyze prey. It is not usually poisonous enough to kill humans and other animals. In some cases, however, it can kill. The most dangerous species of scorpion are found in Africa, the Middle East, Mexico and the United States.

- **At night**, scorpions use the stars to navigate and move around.

- **Scorpions** can store a large amount of food inside their body, which allows them to live without food for up to a year.

▼ *A wood scorpion. Scorpions belong to the most ancient family of arachnids. Like spiders, their bodies are divided into two sections (a cephalothorax and an abdomen) and they have four pairs of legs.*

Giant hairy scorpion

- **Giant hairy scorpions** are among the largest scorpions in North America and have hair all over their bodies.

- **These scorpions** have brown bodies and yellow legs and can be easily recognized.

- **Although** they have very weak eyesight, the hairs on their bodies help them to detect ground and air vibrations and any other movement near them.

- **Giant hairy scorpions** have a long tail, with a bulblike poison gland at the tip. They have large pincers called pedipalps to clasp their prey.

- **Aggressive creatures**, they sting with the slightest provocation. Their sting is painful but not fatal.

- **Giant hairy scorpions** are carnivores and feed on small insects and baby lizards.

- **Mostly found** in desert regions, such as in California and Arizona in the United States, these scorpions can withstand extremely hot weather and are commonly found under rocks. They also burrow into the ground.

- **Giant hairy scorpions** are nocturnal. During the day, they rest to avoid the heat and come out at night to hunt for food or find a mate. They lie in wait to ambush their prey, then they grab it with their pincers.

- **These scorpions** maintain the moisture content in their body by sucking the fluids from their prey.

- **Some people** keep giant hairy scorpions as pets and give them crickets as food.

▼ *Also known as desert hairy scorpions, the giant hairy scorpion prefers dry, hot habitats. It can reach up to 15 cm in length and is able to hunt and catch prey larger than itself.*

Ticks

- **Ticks** are invertebrates, which closely resemble their relatives, the mites. Like mites, they can be found all over the world. Around 850 species of tick are known to exist.

- **Parasitic**, they feed on the blood of mammals, such as humans, dogs and cows.

- **Ticks range** between 0.2 to 0.6 cm in length. They prefer to live in temperate regions, in habitats such as grasslands.

- **Ticks** have a hard outer covering and four pairs of clawed legs. They cannot run, fly or hop as other arachnids can. However, they climb on grass and small plants, as well as on manmade structures, such as walls.

- **The strong sensory organs** of a tick help them to sense the presence of a host so they can be ready to attack.

- **They climb** onto the host and grasp with their legs. Immediately, they sink their mouthparts into the host's skin and start sucking its blood. When they have had enough food, they drop away from the host.

- **Mating** occurs on the host's body itself. After mating, the female tick drops to the ground and lays her eggs. Male ticks usually die after mating.

> ...FASCINATING FACT...
> Ticks can transmit diseases to humans. The deer tick can transmit lyme disease, which causes fever, rashes and swollen joints.

● **There are two major groups** of tick – hard and soft ticks. In a hard tick, the mouth is visible from above. A common example is the American hard tick, which usually feeds on mammals' blood. The female lays many eggs.

● **Soft ticks** have their mouthparts hidden under their body and they mainly feed on the blood of birds. The female soft tick lays fewer eggs than the hard tick.

● **The bite** of a tick causes constant itching, which can persist for months.

▼ *A tick is about the size of a rice grain. Like the mite, it has eight legs and is an arachnid, not an insect. When it has just gorged itself on blood, its baglike body swells up like a balloon.*

Mites

▼ *These tiny creatures are so small that they may be invisible to the naked eye, but they are, nevertheless, an important group of arachnids. Some mites are free-living, others are parasites.*

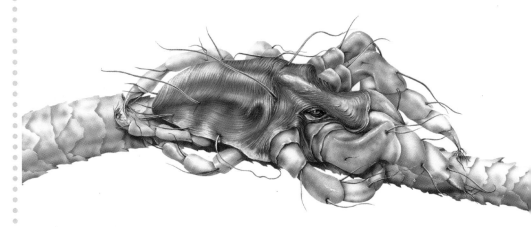

- **Mites** are oval-shaped creatures, which belong to the order Acarina of the class Arachnida. They are found all over the world and around 50,000 species are known to exist.

- **The unsegmented body** of a mite means that the head, thorax and abdomen are fused together. It has four pairs of legs. However, in the larvae stage, it has only three pairs of legs.

- **These insects** have adapted well to both land and water habitats.

- **Mites** breathe through tracheae. These are small, tubelike structures that open on to the surface of their body.

- **Parasitic** creatures, they feed on the blood of a host, which is either a human or another animal. They may be external or internal parasites.

- **The most dangerous pests** for humans and livestock, such as cattle, they carry and transmit serious diseases.

- **Follicle mites** infect human hair roots. Bird mites harm the skin of birds. Chicken mites are known for spreading diseases in poultry.

- **Scabies mites** attack horses, dogs and rabbits and cause itching and bleeding. Some Australian species can also inflict lethal bites.

- **Mites** can also live on vegetation and plant fluids. They cause galllike formations on leaves. Some common plant mites are red spider mites. They spin a web on the undersides of leaves.

FASCINATING FACT
There are certain mites that live in mattresses and pillows, and are carried by dust particles. People use different insecticides and chemicals to try and get rid of them.

Red velvet mite

▼ The red velvet mite searches for bits of fungus and other edible fragments. They are eye-catching arachnids that live in woodlands and gardens. Their beautiful colour warns predators to seek food elsewhere as they taste particularly unpleasant.

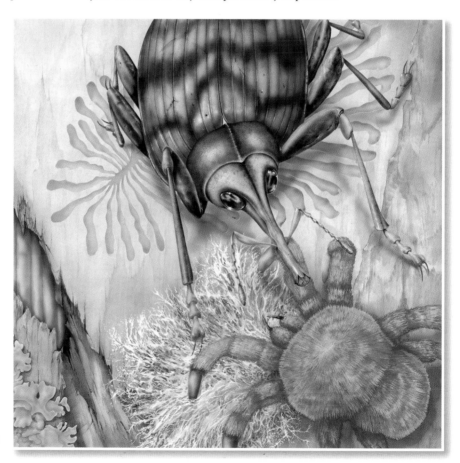

- **Red velvet mites** are soft-bodied. They are usually red to orange in colour and are 1 to 3 mm in length. Their entire body is covered with a fine coat of hair, making it look like velvet.

- **They are** popularly called spider mites. People mistake them for spiders because, like spiders, they spin a loose silk web on the plants they attack.

- **Red velvet mites** have four pairs of legs. Their front legs are used as organs to sense their surroundings.

- **Parasitic** creatures, they feed on the blood of their prey, such as locusts, grasshoppers and crickets. They are known to be voracious predators and feed on insects much bigger than themselves.

- **They usually** live on the bodies of sluggish creatures, where they can suck blood without being disturbed.

- **These small creatures** also attack green foliage. In fact, a red velvet mite attack can cause trees to lose all their leaves.

- **Red velvet mites** are usually spotted during the monsoon season. They can be easily seen in gardens and deciduous woodlands.

- **After mating**, the female lays her eggs in the soil. The eggs hatch quickly and the larvae search for an insect host.

- **Once they** have sucked enough blood from their host, the larvae detach themselves and make a burrow in the soil, where they moult and emerge as adults.

- **Velvet mites** are becoming resistant to pesticides. Therefore, people are developing other ways to control them.

Harvestmen

- **Harvestmen** are often mistaken for spiders. They are not spiders, however, and belong to the order Opiliones.

- **Unlike spiders**, harvestmen do not have spinnerets for secreting the silk thread to make nests and webs.

- **They are called harvestmen** because in Europe, large numbers of them appear in autumn, which is the harvest season.

- **Harvestmen** are usually found in temperate regions of the northern hemisphere and Southeast Asia. About 6000 species of harvestmen are known to exist.

- **They can be spotted** living in hedges, parks, gardens or anywhere near vegetation. They usually gather in large numbers.

- **Harvestmen** have fairly small, oval bodies, usually 4 to 10 mm long. Their bodies look like a single piece and they usually have extremely long, thin legs. Many species do, however, have short, thick legs. Many species are able to shed their legs when they need to escape from their enemies. In some species, the last segment of the leg has many joints, giving it extreme flexibility.

- **Harvestmen** have two eyes in the middle of their head. They appear to be looking sideways.

- **As nocturnal creatures**, they are most active at night. During the day, they hide away from the light by resting under hedgerows or in crevices.

- **Omnivorous insects**, they feed on small insects, insect larvae, and spiders. Certain species also suck the fluids from plant stems as a source of water.

- **They are harmless** and do not have poison glands. They cannot sting.

▲ *At first glance, spiders and harvestmen appear similar. Whereas spiders have two distinct body parts, separated by a waist or stalk, harvestmen have a single, rounded or oval, body shape.*

Schizomids

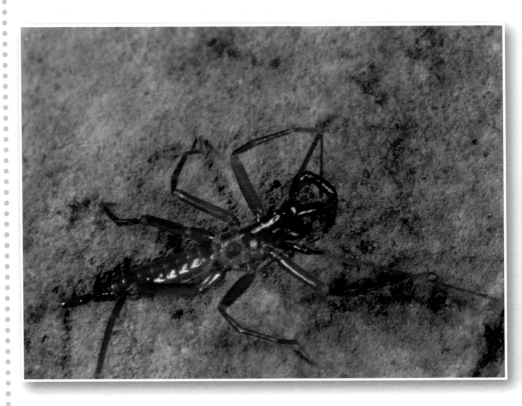

▲ *Little is known about the life cycle and habits of schizomids. These small arachnids avoid light, preferring to live in the damp soil, where they remain hidden from predators.*

- **Schizomids** are small invertebrates (animals without backbones). They belong to the order Schizomida and the class Arachnida.
- **Their name means** 'split or cleaved middle'. Schizomids are named after the front part of their body, which is divided into two separate plates. They are usually about 5 mm long. However, some of them can grow up to 7 mm long.
- **There are about 80** known species of schizomid. These creatures are rare and are found in the tropical and subtropical regions of the world.
- **Schizomids** are pale and silvery and can often be distinguished from other small creatures by their jerky, twitching motion. They have eight legs but use only six legs for walking. The other two legs are used as sensory organs. Schizomids do not have eyes.
- **To catch** their prey, schizomids have two well-developed lobster-like pincers.
- **Carnivorous creatures**, they feed on small insects. They cannot sting and do not have any poison glands.
- **Schizomids** clean themselves regularly with their pincers, bending almost in half to do the job completely.
- **They live under stones**, in leaf litter or in the upper layers of the soil.
- **Males** can easily be distinguished from the females. Females have a short, cylindrical tail, while the males have a more globular tail.
- **After mating**, the females lay their eggs in the soil. They live in underground chambers with their eggs.

Index